The Sun

Steve Parker

WAYLAND

First published in Great Britain in 2007
by Wayland, an imprint of Hachette Children's Books

Hachette Children's Books
338 Euston Road, London NW1 3BH

Editor: Nicola Edwards
Designer: Tim Mayer
Consultant: Ian Graham

British Library Cataloguing in Publication Data
Parker, Steve
   The Sun. - (Earth and space)
   1. Sun - Juvenile literature
   I. Title
   523.7

ISBN-13: 9780750249195

Cover photograph: The Sun's surface 'boils' with fire
and flames.

Photo credits: © Association of Universities for
Research in Astronomy Inc. (AURA), all rights
reserved." "National Optical Astronomy
Observatories, National Science Foundation": 25;
Oliver de Berg/dpa/Corbis: 32; Caterina
Bernadi/zefa/Corbis: 36; Dean Conger/Corbis: 38;
Dagli Orti/Palazzo Pitti Florence/Art Archive: 11b;
Dagli Orti/Templo Mayor Library Mexico/The Art
Archive: 10; Mary Evans PL: 13; David Hardy/ESA: 43;
R. Hurt (SSC/Caltech)/JPL/NASA: 9; Claus Lunau /
FOCI / Bonnier Publications / SPL: 15c; Courtesy
Mount Palomar Observatory/Topfoto: 30; NASA: 5, 6,
7, 8, 14, 15t, 16, 20, 22, 26, 28, 29, 31, 33, 34, 37, 40,
41, 42, 45; NASA/ESA: 18; NOAA: 39; Charles
O'Rear/Corbis: 21; Gabe Palmer/Corbis: 4c; Detlev van
Ravenswaay/SPL: 27; Ross Ressmeyer/Corbis: 24;
Reuters/Corbis: 11t; Bin Sheng/epa/Corbis: 19; Paul A.
Souders/Corbis: 23; Joshua Strang/US
Airforce/ZUMA/Corbis: 35; Superstock: front cover;
Topfoto: 17.Charles Walker/Topfoto: 12, 44.

Contents

Our Local Star

The Sun rules our lives. Every day it gives the world light and warmth, makes our food crops grow, melts snow and puts people in a good mood. Yet this great burning, blinding ball of fire is just one of countless millions of similar objects in space.

Here the Moon is nearly full, which means the Sun shines on almost all of the side we see from Earth.

The Sun's light

On a clear night we see the light from thousands of twinkling stars. On a clear day we see just one star – the Sun. The other stars are still there, but their tiny pinpoints of light are swamped the Sun's incredible brightness. In the Solar System only the Sun makes its own light. We see the planets and moons because they reflect, or bounce back, the Sun's light.

Why the Sun is so big

The Sun looks so big, bright and hot because it is so near. On average, it is about 150 million kilometres from our planet Earth. This is a tiny distance compared to the next nearest star, called Alpha Centauri A, which is 41 million million kilometres away. Nothing travels faster than light, at 300,000 kilometres per second. Light from the Sun takes more than eight minutes to reach Earth. Light from Alpha Centauri A takes more than four years.

Space Facts

Other stars

- The hottest stars, known as group O stars, have a surface temperature at least six times that of the Sun.
- The coolest stars, N and S, are half as hot as the Sun.
- The red supergiant star, Betelgeuse, is 10,000 times brighter than the Sun.
- Betelgeuse is so big that if it was at the centre of our Solar System, the Earth would be inside it, about two-thirds of the way out from its centre.

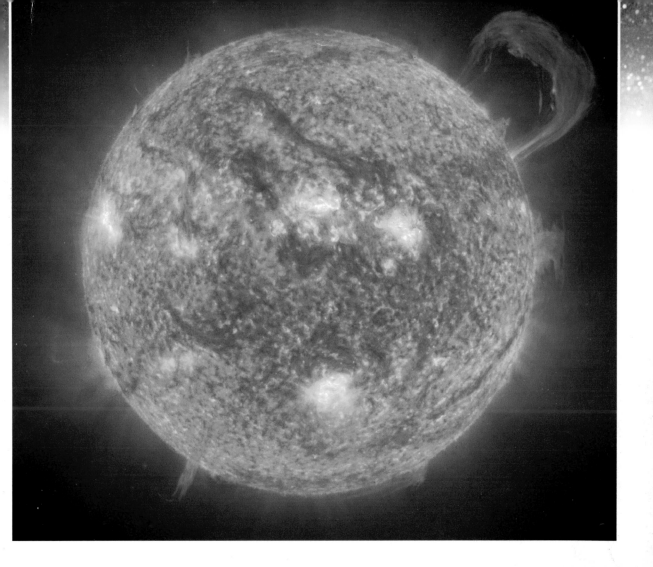

The Sun as a star

Stars are objects in space that give out heat, light and other forms of energy. There are many kinds of stars, from tiny dwarves to colossal supergiants. The Sun seems huge and fierce to us. But compared to other types of stars, it's very average in size, brightness and hotness. It is a type of star known as a G2 dwarf star. There are many billions of Sun-like stars out in deep space.

Seen through a special telescope that darkens it thousands of times, the Sun's surface 'boils' with fire and flames.

How far is the Sun?

The Earth orbits (goes around) the Sun at an average distance of 150 million kilometres, or to be more accurate, 149,597,870 kilometres. This distance is called the Astronomical Unit, AU, and is used to measure distances in space. For example, the planet Venus is 0.72 AU from the Sun – closer to the Sun than we are. The outer planet Neptune is 30 AUs from the Sun – 30 times farther than we are.

How the Sun Began

Immense faint clouds of gas and dust floating in space are known as nebulae, and are places where stars can form.

About five billion (5,000 million) years ago the Sun did not exist. Neither did the planets that go around it, such as Mars, Earth and Jupiter. These objects are part of the Solar System and they all formed at the same time, about 4.5 billion years ago.

Gas and dust
Space is not empty. Apart from stars, planets and other objects, stringy wisps of gas and tiny particles of dust float here and there. A cloud of gas and dust is called a nebula. Nebulae are thought to form when gas and dust are swept together by a nearby star that becomes so big and hot that it explodes.

From cloud to ball
As a nebula shrinks, its particles of matter come closer. This means they pull or attract each other more strongly by the force called gravity. They gather into a tighter lump. Gradually the vast cloud or nebula shrinks into a smaller ball shape and starts to spin. This is the proto-star (meaning first or original star) stage.

Space Facts

The Sun's history
- The Sun probably started to form about 5 billion years ago.
- By 4.5 billion years ago it had started to shine, and the planets were in orbit around it.

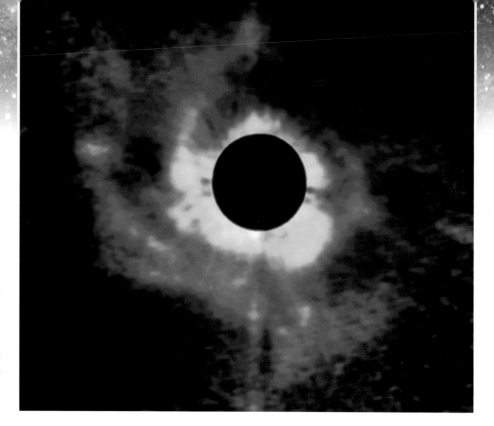

Blocking out the intense light from the very young star AB Aurigae reveals a dim disc of gas and dust around it, which may become planets in millions of years.

Switching on

As the particles get closer they rub and bump each other, increasing the temperature and pressure in the proto-star. When it reaches a certain size the individual particles are so squashed together that they smash into each other. This sets off a chain reaction that releases energy (see page 19). The whirling ball-shaped proto-star 'switches on', gives off light and heat, and becomes a star. This was probably how the Sun began.

Various bits and clouds of dust whirled around the new Sun, in a disc or plate shape. They also started to clump together under their own gravity, forming larger, heavier lumps. Over tens of millions of years these gathered into a few huge lumps that became the planets of the Solar System.

How do we know?

Time travel

Can we go back in time to discover the Sun's history? In a way, yes. Looking through huge telescopes, we see stars in different stages of their 'lives' – forming, growing, fading and exploding. Also, light takes a very long time to reach us from deep space. So when we look at faraway stars and nebulae, we see them as they were millions or billions of years ago. Observing nebulae and stars of different ages, at different distances, shows how our Sun began – and how it will end.

The Sun in the Middle

The Solar System includes the Sun, the planets that go around it, the moons which go around the planets, smaller bits of rock such as asteroids and meteoroids, and occasional glowing, long-tailed visitors called comets. The Sun's immense pulling power, or gravity, keeps the system together.

Every object has a force called gravity that attracts or pulls other objects. The more matter or substance there is in an object, the bigger its force of gravity. Here on our planet we are pulled down onto the ground by Earth's gravity. Its gravity extends into space and pulls on the Moon and the satellites we launch that go around the Earth.

Pulling power

The Sun is at the centre of the Solar System. It is so immense and contains so much matter that its gravity is huge. If you could stand on the Sun's surface, it would pull you down 28 times more powerfully than the Earth does. The Sun's gravity extends to the farthest planets such as Neptune, and beyond – more than 50 times the distance from the Earth to the Sun.

The planets and moons are different sizes, shapes and colours, but all are kept in orbit by the Sun's gigantic pull of gravity.

In orbit

As an object such as a planet travels through space it naturally tries to move in a straight line. But the Sun pulls on it and makes its path curved. The planet's tendency to travel straight exactly balances the Sun's force of gravity making it go in a curve. This is why the planets go round and round the Sun in never-ending orbits.

Scorched by the Sun

The Sun sends out incredible amounts of light, heat and other energy. This affects all the planets. The small planet Mercury is closest to the Sun, only 58 million kilometres away from it. Its surface is blasted by the Sun's heat and reaches temperatures of 400° Celsius – ten times hotter than a scorching day on Earth. The next closest planet, Venus, has thick clouds that trap the Sun's heat. So Venus is even hotter, with a surface temperature of almost 500°C.

Sun

Our Galaxy has billions of stars, with the Sun over halfway from the centre.

The Galaxy

The Sun and whole Solar System are part of a huge whirling cluster of stars and planets called the Milky Way galaxy, or sometimes, the Galaxy (with a capital 'G'). The Sun is about two-thirds of the way out from the Milky Way's centre. The Sun and whole Solar System circle around the centre at almost 220 kilometres per second, taking 225 million years to go around once.

SPACE DATA

The Sun is about:

109 times	wider than Earth.
10 times	wider than even the biggest planet, Jupiter.
1.3 million times	the volume of Earth.
24 million times	the volume of its closest planet, Mercury.

The Sun and the Ancients

Aztec priests offered their Sun god the still-throbbing hearts ripped from living people.

Long ago, many people worshipped the Sun. Before the days of electric lamps and central heating, it was their main source of light and warmth. But gradually the Sun was seen as less of a god, and more as a huge blazing object far away in space, to be studied and understood.

Sun worship

Many ancient people believed that the Sun ruled the skies and the whole world. At night, when the Sun set, it was cold and dark apart from camp fires and candles. At dawn the Sun brought light and heat again. Awed by its power, ancient people made the Sun into a god and invented legends and tales about it. The Ancient Egyptians called their sun god Amon-Re or Ra. The Ancient Greek sun god was Helios, the Ancient Romans used the name Apollo, and the Aztecs of South America had the name Huitzilopochtli.

Sun study

A few people in ancient times were interested in the science of the Sun, rather than religion and worship. Almost 2,600 years ago the Greek thinker Anaximander studied the Sun's movements across the sky using a sundial, an instrument with a flat surface and an upright pointer that casts a shadow. As the Sun moves across the sky the pointer's shadow moves too. Marks on the flat surface show roughly the time of day and season. Anaximander found how the length of daylight varied through the year, being longest in mid summer and shortest in mid winter.

Threat of death

More than 2,400 years ago Anaxagoras of Greece suggested the Sun was made of burning rocks or metal, rather than being some kind of god or spirit in a fiery chariot. But most people saw this idea as crazy and insulting to the gods, and Anaxagoras was threatened with death.

The massive monument of Stonehenge in west England was both a temple for worship and sacrifice, and a calendar to plan events.

Then about 2,300 years ago the Greek astronomer Aristarchus suggested that the Earth went around the Sun. Again, most people believed that the Earth was the centre of everything, and laughed at Aristarchus. More than 1,800 years later he was shown to be right.

The Sun and calendars

The Sun's motion through space helped many people in ancient times to work out calendars showing days and years. From about 5,000 years ago in Britain people made the great stone circle of Stonehenge, as a temple and calendar. Its pattern of stones lines up with the Sun's rise on midsummer day. The Mayan people of Central America made accurate calendars from about 1,700 to 1,000 years ago, to help them plan crop planting and days of worship.

Early Science of the Sun

This is an early illustration of the Earth going around the Sun, as suggested by Copernicus.

The invention of the telescope in about 1608 brought the Sun, Moon, planets and stars much closer. Astronomers could now study the Sun's surface by shining its image onto a card or by using special very dark filters on their telescopes. They could see the Sun blazing fiercely (although for some this caused sight problems or even lost them their sight).

A Sun-centred system

One of the first scientists to aim a telescope at the skies was Galileo Galilei, in Italy in 1609-10. He had read the ideas of Polish astronomer Nicolaus Copernicus, whose book of 1543 suggested that the Earth and other planets went around the Sun. At the time most people, including most scientists, believed that the Earth was at the centre of everything. Anyone who went against this belief, called the geocentric system, risked prison or even death.

Galileo's studies gradually showed other astronomers that the heliocentric version, with the Sun at the centre of the Solar System, was correct. Galileo also observed sunspots and how they moved, showing that the Sun, like the Earth, spins around.

Space fact

The Astronomical Unit

● In 1672 astronomers made the first fairly accurate measurement of the Sun's distance from Earth (the astronomical unit, AU). Their estimate was 140 million kilometres, which was only 10 million kilometres too low.

As Galileo explained the new telescope to his colleagues, many thought it was for spying on enemy armies rather than gazing at stars.

Clues in sunlight

In 1812-14 German scientist and telescope maker Joseph von Fraunhofer was working on some new designs for the curved pieces of glass called lenses. He shone sunlight through a combination of thin slits, lenses and triangular pieces of glass called prisms. This split the sunlight into different colours, called the solar spectrum. (We see this when raindrops do the same, as the colours of the rainbow.)

Von Fraunhofer noticed that there were dark lines or stripes in certain parts of the Sun's spectrum. In 1859 German scientist Gustav Kirchhoff worked out that these lines showed what the Sun was made of. The position of each line indicated a certain type of substance or chemical in the Sun. The lines became known as Fraunhofer lines. They are still studied today in the light from the Sun and other stars.

How do we know?

Bending light

In 1915 the great scientist Albert Einstein came up with his theory of relativity. One of its predictions was that light passing close to a star would bend, due to the star's huge pull of gravity. In 1919 British space expert Arthur Eddington travelled to West Africa to study an eclipse of the Sun (see pages 32-33). He saw that light from distant stars was indeed bent as it went past another star – the Sun.

The Sun's Size and Shape

After about 400 years of scientific study, we now know a great amount about the Sun. Experts have measured its size and shape, and how it spins around. Every few years these measurements become more accurate as scientists develop better equipment such as bigger telescopes and new satellites.

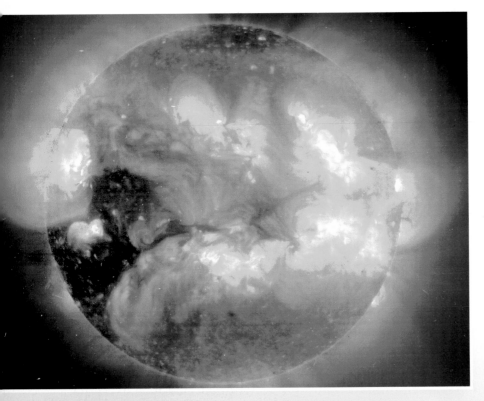

This SOHO picture of the Sun shows not light waves, but slightly shorter waves called ultraviolet rays.

Nearly a perfect ball

The planets of the Solar System, like Jupiter, Mars and Earth itself, are usually described as spheres – that is, ball-shaped. In fact most are not exact spheres. They are squashed slightly from top to bottom. The Sun is not. It is much more spherical, or perfectly ball shaped.

The Sun's diameter – the distance from one side to the other – is 1,392,000 kilometres. This is quite a difficult measurement to make because the Sun's surface has huge flames that flare up and then die down. This makes the diameter slightly bigger or smaller through time. The Sun's surface area is just over six million million square kilometres. This is nearly 12,000 times the surface area of Earth.

How do we know?
SOHO's studies

The *SOHO* satellite studies the Sun in great detail. Its name means Solar and Heliospheric Observatory and it is about 1.5 million kilometres from Earth towards the Sun. It was launched in 1995 and still sends back new pictures and information about the Sun every day.

The car-sized SOHO satellite has solar panels nearly 10 metres across, that turn sunlight into electricity.

Mass of the Sun

Mass is the amount of substance or matter in an object. On Earth we call it 'weight'. The Sun's mass is almost 2,000 billion billion billion tonnes. This is nearly one-third of a million times more than the Earth's mass. The Sun is about 1,000 times the mass – 1,000 times heavier – than all the planets and all their moons combined.

Spinning Sun

Like the Earth, the Sun twirls around like a giant spinning top. But it does not turn like a solid ball. The Sun is made mainly of gases and other substances which are 'floppy'. Different parts of it spin at different speeds. Around the Sun's middle, or equator, the surface travels at 7,200 kilometres per hour. This part of the Sun turns around once every 25 to 26 days. Deep inside, underneath the equator, the spin speed is faster. Away from the equator, towards the upper and lower parts of the Sun, the spin speed is slower. The top and bottom of the Sun turn around once every 37 days.

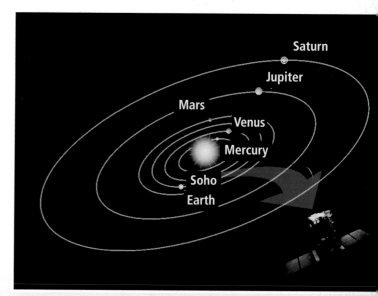

SOHO's orbit is inside Earth's orbit, so our planet never blocks its view of the Sun.

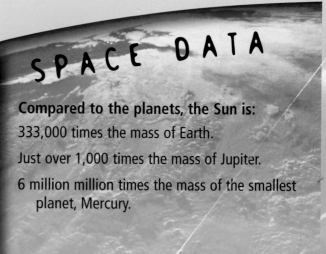

SPACE DATA

Compared to the planets, the Sun is:

333,000 times the mass of Earth.

Just over 1,000 times the mass of Jupiter.

6 million million times the mass of the smallest planet, Mercury.

15

The Structure of the Sun

Convective zone

Photosphere (visible surface)

Radiative zone

Core

No spacecraft has been very close to the Sun, let alone landed on its flaming surface. What we know about the Sun's interior has been worked out from many kinds of information. This includes the amount of light and heat given off, the exact colours in sunlight, and experiments here on Earth that try to 'copy' the incredible temperatures and pressures in different parts of the Sun.

From the outside in

The Sun has six main layers. The surface layer that we see and study through special telescopes is called the photosphere. It is not solid like rock, but made of energy escaping from the Sun like blazing flames. When we measure the size of the Sun, it is to the outer surface of the photosphere.

A cutaway view of the Sun shows its inner layers and the very thin surface layer, the photosphere, with its speckle-like sunspots.

SPACE DATA

Imagine the Sun could shrink down to just 100 centimetres (one metre) across – the size of a very big beachball. Its layers would be:

Photosphere –	less than 1 millimetre thick.
Convective zone –	about 25 centimetres thick.
Radiative zone –	about 50 centimetres thick.
Core –	about 50 centimetres across (diameter).

The Sun is mainly hydrogen, which burns very easily. It was used to fill airships – until the terrible Hindenburg disaster in 1937.

We cannot see through the photosphere. But it's thought that underneath there are three more layers. Going towards the centre of the Sun these are called the convective zone, the radiative zone and, at the centre, the core. The convective and radiative zones are so named as they describe the way in which energy travels through them.

Above the surface

Above the photosphere is the chromosphere. This is the 'atmosphere' that surrounds the Sun in a similar way to the see-through layer of air that forms the atmosphere around Earth. The outermost layer of the Sun is known as the corona. It is thin and wispy and extends huge distances into space.

How do we know?
What is the Sun made of?

By studying the energy and colours in sunlight, along with the lines called Fraunhofer lines (see page 13), scientists have worked out what the Sun is made of.

● About three-quarters of the Sun is made of the lightest known substance, hydrogen. (Hydrogen was used to fill giant airships but it catches fire easily and so is very dangerous.)

● Almost one-quarter is the second-lightest substance, helium. (We use it on Earth to fill party balloons.)

● About 1/130th is oxygen, the vital gas in air we breathe to stay alive.

● There are also tiny amounts of carbon, iron, neon, nitrogen, silicon, magnesium and sulphur.

At the Heart of the Sun

The Sun is sometimes said to be a ball of burning gas. But that's not quite the case – in fact, it's neither solid, liquid or gas. In the middle of the Sun is the core, a vast ball-shaped mass which produces light, heat and other forms of energy. Scientists are fairly sure how this happens, but there are still some mysteries to solve.

Plasma

Most of the substances or matter inside the Sun are not really in the form of gas, in the way that gases such as nitrogen and oxygen make up the air around us. Neither is the Sun solid or liquid. It is made of a fourth form, or state, of matter. This is called plasma.

This TRACE satellite view shows a pale burst of plasma leaving the Sun.

Most substances, if heated enough, change into plasma. A plasma can change shape and move, like a gas. But its tiniest particles are not atoms, which make up other forms of matter. In a plasma the atoms fall apart slightly. They exist as the central parts of atoms, called nuclei, separate from the outer parts, known as electrons.

SPACE DATA

The Sun's core

● The core of the Sun is about 350,000 kilometres across.

● Its temperature is up to 15 million degrees C.

● Its pressure is 300 billion times the air pressure around us at sea level here on Earth.

● A cupful of the Sun's core would weigh 100 times the same-sized cupful of water on Earth.

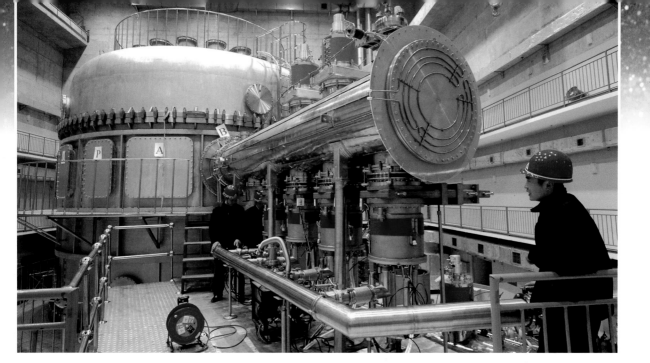

Scientists have copied the Sun's energy-making nuclear changes here on Earth, in fusion reactors called tokomaks. These may be able to provide us with power in the future.

Matter to energy

Most of the plasma in the Sun's core is hydrogen. The temperature is so hot, and the crushing force of gravity is so great, that the nuclei of hydrogen are sometimes squeezed together. As this happens they form heavier substances, mainly helium. Usually four nuclei of hydrogen atoms join or fuse to make one nucleus of a helium atom. This happens untold billions of times every second inside the Sun, and is called nuclear fusion.

The helium nucleus is lighter – that is, it has less mass – than the four hydrogen nuclei. The difference in mass becomes energy, chiefly heat and light, and also other forms such as gamma rays and X-rays. As the Sun changes matter to energy it gradually becomes lighter, by about 4.3 million tonnes every second.

Space Fact

The Sun's power

● A very powerful explosive on Earth is TNT. When one tonne of TNT blows up it can destroy several buildings. Energy production in the Sun is the same as 96 million billion tonnes of TNT per second.

Does the Sun 'burn'?

As well as being mostly plasma rather than gas, the Sun does not really burn. When we burn something on Earth, it combines with the gas oxygen in the air to give out heat and light, as flames. There is no air and hardly any oxygen in the Sun. The heat and light look like fire and flames. But they are made by nuclear fusion, not by burning.

The Sun's Inner Layers

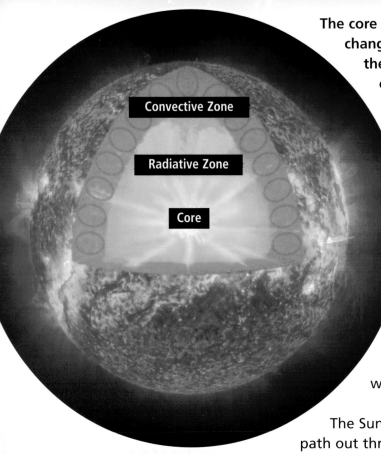

Convective Zone

Radiative Zone

Core

Energy takes thousands of years to pass out of the Sun.

The core is the only part of the Sun that changes matter into energy. The energy then begins its journey away from the core. It takes a long time to pass through the inner layers, the radiative zone and the convective zone.

Radiative zone

The radiative zone extends from the core to about three-quarters of the way to the Sun's surface. Energy travels out through it in the form of radiation, or rays. We are familiar with energy travelling as waves or rays of radiation here on Earth, such as radio waves, microwaves, light waves and X-rays.

The Sun's energy does not follow a straight path out through the radiative zone. The plasma is so hot and squashed that the rays bounce and zig-zag around. It probably takes one small 'packet' of energy almost 200,000 years to pass from the core through the radiative zone to the next layer.

Convective zone

In the convective zone, the plasma is not quite so heated and crushed as in the radiative zone. The Sun's energy travels in a different way, being carried by 'lumps' or 'bubbles' of plasma that flow. These flows of energy are called convection currents.

SPACE DATA

The Sun's zones
- The radiative zone is about 350,000 kilometres thick.

- The convective zone is about 170,000 kilometres thick.

- However both these measurements are scientific guesses. Some experts say that the convective zone is nearer 200,000 kilometres deep.

We see convection currents in a small way when we boil water, and the water swirls and bubbles as it carries the heat. The same happens when a tarmac roadway warms in the Sun and passes heat energy to the air above, which rises and causes a wavy, shimmering pattern.

Space Facts

The Sun's power

- The temperature in the Sun falls with distance from the core.
- Near the inside of the radiative zone the temperature is probably about 12 million degrees C.
- Near the outside of the convective zone it is less that 2 million degrees C. Scientists have created temperatures hotter than this here on Earth. In one experiment in 1994 at the Princeton Plasma Physics Laboratory, New Jersey, USA, plasma was heated to more than 500 million degrees C.

In the Sun a convection current picks up energy from the radiative zone beneath, travels outwards, releases its energy into the Sun's surface, cools and sinks, and then does the same again. These currents happen all around the convective zone and carry the heat and light much faster than through the radiative zone.

We see convection on Earth when heat-carrying air currents above a hot road make it shimmer.

The Sun's Surface

The surface layer of the Sun is called the photosphere. It seems to boil with flames as the heat, light and other energy leave the Sun and start their journey into space. They travel at the fastest speed in the Universe – the speed of light.

Boiling bright

The photosphere is where the Sun's plasma and gas become so thin and spread out that light and the other forms of radiation can escape into space. The convection, or carrying, of heat up through the convective zone gives the Sun its 'boiling' appearance. Its surface looks mottled or patchy all over, which is an appearance known as granular. Why is this?

Granules and supergranules

As a convection current or cell reaches the photosphere it forms an extra-bright area called a granule, which is usually about 1,000 kilometres across. As this loses heat its plasma and gas cool slightly by about 300 degrees C. They form a slightly duller area around the bright granule. The cooled gas and plasma sink back into the convective zone, where they pick up more heat and rise again.

The brighter spots on the Sun caused by heat rising are known as granules.

Sometimes many granules merge to form a supergranule which could be as big as 30,000 kilometres across. The flows of plasma and gas in the granules and supergranules move up and down at speeds of 300-500 kilometres every second.

Limb darkening

One feature of the Sun is called limb darkening. When looking at the Sun's disc, it is slightly darker towards and around the edges than in the middle. This is due to the thickness of the photosphere and the way its temperature falls. The bottom of the photosphere is around 6,850 degrees C, while its top is cooler at 4,650 degrees C. This means we look at the hottest region of it when viewing the middle of the Sun, and cooler regions when we view the Sun almost side-on, around the edges of its disc.

Molten (melted) metal looks incredibly hot, yet it is far cooler than the Sun's surface.

A Halo Around the Sun

Above the boiling surface of the Sun is a layer of gases called the chromosphere. Beyond this is the Sun's outermost layer, the very large, thin and wispy corona. Both of these layers are transparent, so we can see through them to the photosphere surface.

The chromosphere

On Earth, above the surface we have a layer of air – a mix of see-through gases called the atmosphere. This fades away gradually into space. The corona is a layer of gases that forms the Sun's atmosphere. It extends above the Sun's surface about 25 times higher than our own atmosphere extends above the Earth.

The name chromosphere means 'coloured ball'. This is because the chromosphere can be seen as a flash of reddish colour, just before and after a total eclipse of the Sun (see page 32-33).

The corona

The faint, thin, wispy gases and plasma of the corona ('crown') extend from the top of the chromosphere, out into space for millions of kilometres.

With the Sun's super-bright disc blocked, the corona shows as a glow all around.

Spicules are long, thin squirts of incredibly hot gas, each one as tall as the Earth, shooting up from the Sun's surface.

They gradually fade away into the emptiness of space. During an eclipse of the Sun the corona shows as a vast, faint glow all around the Sun, about one million times less bright than the Sun itself.

Hotter and hotter

From the centre of the Sun to the surface, or photosphere, the temperature falls. But from the photosphere up into the corona it begins to rise again. It reaches about 30,000 degrees C by the top of the chromosphere. Puzzlingly, the temperature continues to rise in the corona, and may reach 3.5 million degrees C. Why this happens is still something of a mystery.

Scattered through the corona are coronal 'holes' where the plasma and gases are cooler and thinner. They are most common over the Sun's poles (its top and bottom). Why these form is also puzzling scientists.

Spicules

Spicules are streaky, sharp, spike-like jets of gas that shoot outwards from the photosphere, up through the chromosphere into the corona. A typical spicule is about 10,000 kilometres tall and around 1,000 kilometres wide, and lasts for 5-10 minutes. Its temperature is probably about 15,000 degrees C. When many spicules happen together near each other, they look like a patch of 'fur' on the Sun's surface.

How do we know?

The corona

For many years, scientists did not understand why the Sun's corona is so vast. Calculations showed it should be much smaller. Then, in 1940, the American physicist William Lamb studied its light and found that its temperature was very high, million of degrees. This explained why the corona extends so far. The next mystery is to explain why the corona is so hot.

Sunspots and Solar Flares

The Sun's surface is never still. Apart from its steady 'boiling', various kinds of flame-like, superheated blasts of gas and plasma explode or hurl themselves into space. There are also darker patches on the surface. These features help to explain what is happening inside the Sun.

Spotty Sun

For more than 2,000 years, people have noticed slightly darker regions on the Sun's surface, known as sunspots. They regularly appear and then fade. They are darker than the surrounding photosphere because they are slightly cooler – although their temperature is still a super-scorching 5,000 degrees C. The darkest centre of a sunspot is the umbra, and the slightly lighter area around it is the penumbra.

Sunspots vary in size and usually form in groups.

Sunspots occur in a wide range of sizes. Many are about 10,000 to 20,000 kilometres across – wider than the Earth. They usually occur in pairs, and form in groups of up to 10. They seem to move across the Sun's disc, and this is because the Sun turns around. Most sunspots last a few weeks. A few are there for several months. They are probably caused by very powerful regions of the Sun's magnetism (see page 30).

Small, extra-bright patches of the photosphere are called faculae. They are even hotter than the rest of the photosphere. Often a facula forms first, and then becomes darker, turning into a sunspot in the same place.

How do we know?

Studying sunspots

In the 1840s German astronomer Heinrich Schwabe noticed that sunspots and other surface features varied over time. He saw that they changed from being small and scarce, to bigger and more numerous, then faded away again, over an 11-year period. This sunspot cycle was also studied in detail by the *SolarMax* satellite in the 1980s (see page 36).

Solar flares

A solar flare is a massive outburst of energy that looks like a huge flame leaping up from the Sun's surface, through the chromosphere and into the corona. The biggest flares are millions of kilometres long and usually happen near sunspots. As they grow over several minutes they are up to 10 times brighter than the surrounding surface. Then they fade away over the following hours. Some solar flares are like volcanoes. They erupt and spray huge amounts of hot gas and plasma into space. They also give out bursts of radiation or wave energy, including radio waves (see page 31).

(see page 31)

Space Facts

Sunpots and solar flares

● In 2001 the *SOHO* satellite took pictures of a huge sunspot group 13 times bigger than the Earth.

● If we could capture all the energy in one solar flare, it would be enough to power all our machines, engines and vehicles here on Earth for half a million years.

Solar flares curve up around the Sun's very strong magnetism, and loop back down to its surface.

Arches and Loops

Apart from granules, sunspots and flares, the Sun has even more gigantic features on its surface. These are called solar filaments and prominences. There are also great outbursts of gas which are thrown away from the Sun, called Coronal Mass Ejections (CMEs).

Flares and filaments

The Sun's magnetism is very powerful. Gas and plasma tend to collect and move along its lines of magnetic force. If these magnetic forces curve up above the Sun's surface, flaming tongues of gas and plasma travel along them. The magnetism may loop up and down again, producing what looks like an 'arch of fire'.

These features are called solar prominences or solar filaments, depending on how we see them. If they occur over the disc of the Sun, we see them against the background of the photosphere surface.

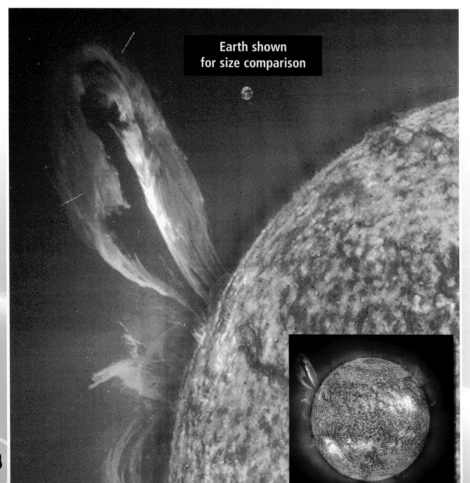

Earth shown
for size comparison

An arch prominence would dwarf planet Earth, which is drawn at the same scale for comparison.

How do we know?
Studying solar flares

Satellites have been launched from Earth to allow scientists to study the various features of the Sun. For example, *RHESSI* is a small satellite launched in 2002. It is designed especially to study solar flares. It can detect many kinds of high-energy waves, including gamma rays and X-rays. Its name means Reuven Ramaty High Energy Solar Spectroscopic Imager. (Reuven Ramaty was a famous expert on the Sun.)

They show up as streaky lines called solar filaments, slightly darker and cooler than the photosphere below. If they occur at the edge of the Sun we see them side-on. They look like massive curls or loops of flame jumping out from the Sun's edge, called solar prominences.

If a solar prominence throws heat and other energy away from the Sun, it is called eruptive. If it simply 'hangs' above the surface for days or weeks, then fades away, it is known as a quiescent prominence.

CMEs

Coronal mass ejections are colossal 'bubbles' of gas and plasma that float away from the Sun over a few hours. They are probably caused by changes in the incredibly powerful magnetic forces within and around the Sun. Flares, filaments and CMEs all send out bursts of radio waves.

Space Facts

Solar prominences

● Solar prominences look like solar flares but are larger and longer-lasting.

● A typical prominence is thousands of kilometres long.

● The largest ones are half a million kilometres tall, and can arch up and down to another part of the Sun half a million kilometres away.

● The temperature inside a solar prominence can be higher than 70,000 degrees C.

The RHESSI satellite is about 2 metres tall and spins around every four seconds, yet stays pointing straight at the Sun.

The Sun as a Magnet

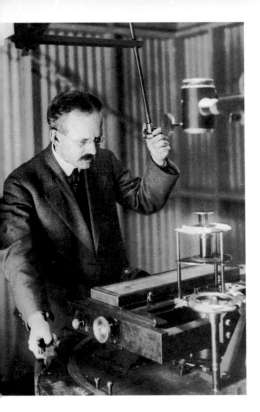

George Ellery Hale helped to establish three observatories – Yerkes, Mount Wilson and Palomar.

Most of the planets, including Earth, have a magnetic field. Invisible lines of magnetic force curve up from our North Pole, around the planet and down into the South Pole. We can detect Earth's magnetic field with a magnetic compass and use it to find our way. The Sun has a magnetic field too, but it is much more powerful and complicated than Earth's.

Electricity and magnetism

The superheated plasma and gases of the Sun carry electricity very well. As they whirl around in the Sun, they make electrical energy, like a spinning generator in a power station. Wherever there is electricity, there is also magnetism. The two occur together as one of the most basic or fundamental forces in the Universe, known as electromagnetism.

A magnetic doughnut

Different parts of the Sun turn at different speeds (see page 15). This sets up differences in the magnetic field. The Earth's magnetic forces run from pole to pole, north to south (top to bottom). Some of the Sun's lines of magnetic force do the same. But others run east to west, around the Sun. All together, the lines make a magnetic field shaped something like a giant doughnut.

How do we know?
Magnetic fields

American astronomer George Ellery Hale worked out that during an 11-year cycle, on the top half of the Sun the sunspots have their magnetic fields pointing the same way, such as north to the west (left). On the bottom half, the fields are reversed. But after a cycle, all the magnetic lines reverse or 'flip'. All the norths becomes south, the souths becomes north, and another 11-year cycle begins.

Magnetic forces

As the lines of magnetic force change and cross each other in the spinning Sun, they have huge effects. A sunspot is like a 'mini-magnet' on the surface. It has its own very strong magnetic field, with a pole (concentration of magnetic lines) at each end. Solar prominences tend to follow lines of magnetism that arch above the surface.

Crackles and fuzz

The various active Sun features – filaments, prominences, CMEs, sunspots and flares – can produce wave energy, including radio waves and microwaves. These may reach Earth and affect our radio and television, causing crackling sounds and fuzzy pictures. This type of interference is often blamed on 'magnetic storms' on the Sun. It rises and falls with the 11-year cycle of activity. It peaks during the middle of the cycle at a time called the solar maximum, and fades away at the start and end, known as the solar minimum.

Intense magnetism in a sunspot guides heat and light energy in curved paths known as sunspot loops.

31

Eclipses and Transits

The Sun sends its heat and light to Earth all the time – except during a solar eclipse. This is when the Moon comes between the Earth and the Sun. The places on Earth that experience the eclipse become darker and cooler, as the Sun's energy is blocked for a short while. (In a similar way, the Earth comes between the Sun and the Moon in a lunar eclipse, and the Sun's energy cannot reach the Moon.)

How do we know?

Eclipse-chasers

Eclipses provide scientists with very useful opportunities to study the Sun. With the blinding disc of the Sun blotted out by the Moon, the corona appears around the Sun as a pale glow. It's possible to see details of solar flares, prominences and other features since these are usually swamped by the photosphere's brilliant light. Even the chromosphere may be seen as a brief flash of colour. Scientists travel around the world to view eclipses, taking telescopes and other equipment (see page 13).

Eclipsing the Sun

The Sun is far more gigantic than the Moon. But it is also much farther away. From our viewpoint on Earth, the Sun and the Moon appear to be almost the same size. A solar eclipse happens when the Moon eclipses, or passes in front of, the Sun.

Three types of eclipse

There are three main types of solar eclipse. In a partial eclipse the Earth, Moon and Sun are not quite exactly in line. The Moon passes across part of the Sun. It hides some, but not all, of the Sun's disc. So the Sun appears like a curved crescent if mostly hidden, or if the coverage is less, as though someone has bitten a lump out of it.

In this partial eclipse the Moon is passing almost underneath the Sun, to hide only a small part of it.

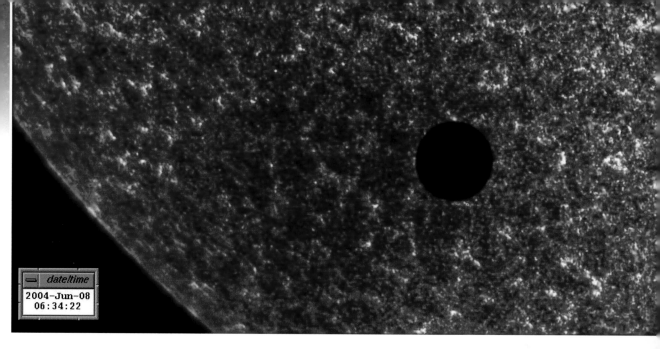

date/time
2004-Jun-08
06:34:22

In a total eclipse the Earth, Moon and Sun are exactly in line. The Moon covers the Sun completely for a short time. However it does not cast a huge shadow over the whole Earth. It casts a small, round, dark, spot-like shadow called the umbra. This moves along the Earth's surface as the Moon orbits the Earth and the Earth itself spins. A total eclipse is only visible from places on Earth in the path of the umbra. On either side of the path is a lesser shadow, the penumbra. People in this area see a partial eclipse.

In 2004 planet Venus passed in front of the Sun, looking like a tiny black spot. It was the first time this was seen from Earth in more than 120 years.

The Moon's orbit around Earth is not an exact circle. So at certain times the Moon is farther from the Earth and looks smaller. When an eclipse happens at this time, the Moon does not quite cover all of the Sun. The result is an annular eclipse, with the outer edge of the Sun visible as a bright ring all around the Moon.

Transits

A transit happens when one object in space passes across the face of another. The two planets nearer to the Sun than us are Mercury and Venus. Now and again they pass across the Sun's disc when viewed from Earth, looking like tiny dark dots. Studying the way sunlight changes as it grazes these planets gives clues to the planets' surfaces, and the atmosphere of Venus, as well as the make-up of sunlight itself.

Space Facts

Solar eclipses

- On average, there are between 2 and 5 solar eclipses each year.

- A total eclipse can only be seen by people in the darkest part of the Moon's shadow, the umbra. The umbra is about 270 kilometres wide.

- A total eclipse lasts about 7 minutes.

The Solar Wind

The Sun sends out many kinds of radiation or rays, such as light and heat. It also gives off particles in the form of the gas-like substance called plasma, into space all around. These particles are the solar wind.

For two and a half years the Genesis probe held out large dish-like collectors to gather particles of the solar wind.

Electrons and protons

The solar wind comes from the Sun's outermost layer, the corona. The main particles are the outer bits of atoms, known as electrons, and the inner pieces or nuclei of hydrogen atoms, called protons. These have both electrical and magnetic forces. They flow continually away from the Sun, as the solar wind. The wind 'blows' out from the Sun in all directions, across the Solar System and beyond.

Wind of change

Sometimes action on the Sun disturbs or adds to the solar wind. One example is the release of huge bubble-like lumps of gas and plasma known as CMEs (see page 29). So the solar wind is not steady. It becomes stronger and weaker with time, and it does not 'blow' with the same strength in all directions.

Measuring the solar wind

The first accurate measurements of the solar wind were made in 1959 by the space probe *Luna 1*. This was the first craft to leave the Earth and head out towards the Moon. Since then many satellites and space probes have studied the wind, including the recent *Genesis* craft (see page 35).

When the wind blows

The solar wind has several effects on and around Earth. Our planet's whole magnetic field, called the magnetosphere, extends far out into space. It would be like a huge ball around the Earth.

Space Facts

Solar wind particles

● The particles of the solar wind can travel at speeds of up to 1,000 kilometres per second. At this speed they would take nearly two days to reach Earth.

● By the time they arrive the particles are travelling between 300 and 700 kilometres per second.

But the electrical-magnetic particles of the solar wind blow against it and make it lopsided. They flatten it on the side nearest the Sun. They make it longer and more pointed on the other, downwind side. So the whole magnetosphere is pear-shaped.

Curtains of light

The solar wind's particles bash into atoms of air high above the Earth's surface. These collisions happen mostly where the Earth's magnetism is strongest, near the North and South Poles, and they make light. They produce glowing, shimmering 'curtains' high in the sky. These are the Northern and Southern Lights, or Aurora Borealis and Aurora Australis.

Northern and Southern Lights glow as the solar wind hits the Earth's magnetic field.

35

The Sun and Life on Earth

The Earth teems with living things – and almost all of this life depends on the Sun. Sunlight gives energy to plants, and plants are the basic food for all animals. Also the heat from the Sun keeps our planet at a suitable temperature, rather than frozen or baking hot.

Plant power

Every living thing needs energy to survive, grow and produce young. Plants get their energy from the Sun. They soak up sunlight in their leaves and 'capture' the energy contained in it. This energy is combined with minerals from the soil, and the gas carbon dioxide from the air, to make the plants' food. The whole process is called photosynthesis, which means 'building with light'.

A sunny day feels warm and comfortable, and also fuels trees and other plants with the solar light energy they need to live and grow.

Energy chains

Animals called herbivores eat the plants and take in their food energy to use for themselves. Animals known as carnivores eat the herbivores or each other and, in turn, take in the energy. So the Sun's light energy passes along food chains, from plants to herbivores to carnivores. These are not just food chains, but energy chains too. If there was no Sun, none of this could happen.

How do we know?
Studying the Sun's energy

The *SolarMax* spacecraft was launched in 1980 to measure energy sent out by the Sun. Its name comes from 'solar maximum', because it studied the Sun at its busiest – the time of the most sunspots, flares and other activities. It found out more details especially about solar flares (see page 26) and the types of energy they give off, not just light and heat but X-rays and gamma rays. Unfortunately the craft went wrong in 1981, but it was rescued and mended by the Space Shuttle *Challenger*. It finally fell back to Earth and burned up in 1989.

Four years into its mission the SolarMax satellite was 'grabbed' by the robot arm of the space shuttle, and repaired by astronauts.

Earth's temperature

The average temperature of the Earth is about 14-15 degrees C. The warmth comes from the Sun in the form of radiation or rays of heat, known as infra-red rays. Without the Sun's heat, our planet would be totally frozen. However the Earth's air or atmosphere helps too. The atmosphere works like an invisible blanket around the planet to allow in the Sun's warmth, and then prevent some of it from leaking back into space. This trapping of heat is called the natural greenhouse effect.

Too warm

In recent times, human activities such as burning fuels have changed the natural greenhouse effect and made it more effective. The atmosphere is starting to trap more and more of the Sun's warmth. This is leading to the massive threat of global warming. Ice-caps could melt and sea levels rise, flooding vast areas of land where millions of people live.

Space Fact

The solar constant

● The solar constant is the name given to the total energy reaching a certain area of the Earth's surface from the Sun in a particular time. Scientists measure changes in the solar constant and link it to the Sun's activities, like the number of solar flares. This helps our understanding of how the Sun makes and sends out its energy.

The energy is in the form of rays or radiation, not only heat and light, but also weak amounts of radio waves, microwaves, ultra-violet rays, X-rays and gamma rays.

How we Observe the Sun

No one should ever look straight at the Sun. Its light is so powerful that it can damage our eyes in a second or two, and easily make us blind. People have been watching the Sun from here on Earth for thousands of years, but using special equipment for their studies.

Early methods

Early Sun-gazing was carried out by various means, such as looking through hazy cloud or partly see-through natural 'mineral glass' such as silica, or by observing the Sun's reflection in a polished surface or a pool of water. Sunspots were first mentioned by astronomers in China more than 2,000 years ago.

The Sun through a telescope

The first studies through telescopes were made by Galileo and other scientists from about 1609-10. Smoked-glass or tinted lenses made the Sun much duller, to protect eyesight. Another method, still used today, is to shine or project the image of the Sun from a telescope onto a screen or card. In a coronagraph a dark disc blots out the blinding main disc of the Sun, as in a total solar eclipse. Only the chromosphere and corona around the edges are visible.

The image of the Sun from the giant McMath-Pierce Telescope is shone onto a surface for study.

How do we know?

Tracking the Sun's movement

The movement of the Sun is tracked by the McMath-Pierce Solar Telescope's curved bowl-like mirror which measures 203 centimetres across. The curved mirror sends the light down a shaft almost 100 metres long buried at an angle into the mountainside, to another mirror at the bottom. This lower mirror bounces the light to a third mirror about halfway back up the shaft. The third mirror sends the light into various detectors and other equipment, for study and viewing. The telescope forms an image of the Sun about 80 centimetres across. It allows scientists to gather a range of information, for example about sunspot patterns, solar flares and solar prominences.

Solar telescopes

The first telescope built specially to study the Sun was the McMath-Pierce Solar Telescope in 1962, at Kitt Peak National Solar Observatory, Arizona, USA. There are also specialized Sun-gazing telescopes at another National Solar Observatory on Sacramento Peak near Cloudcroft, New Mexico, USA. These telescopes look at the range of colours and dark lines in sunlight (see page 13). This gives information about the chemical make-up of the Sun and how fast it is changing its hydrogen into helium and other substances.

Rays and waves

'Ordinary' or optical telescopes receive light waves. Other kinds of telescopes pick up other rays and waves, such as radio waves, microwaves, infra-red or 'heat' rays, ultraviolet waves, X-rays and gamma waves – and the Sun sends out all of these. The information from such telescopes is changed by computers into pictures and lists of numbers, for scientists to study.

This coronagraph telescope is at the Mauna Loa Solar Observatory, 3,440 metres high on the volcanic mountain of Mauna Loa, on the Pacific island of Hawaii.

Space facts

Neutrinos

● Neutrinos are particles smaller than atoms. They are so small, they can pass through almost any object, including the human body, without harm.

● The Sun sends out countless neutrinos. About one million of them pass through you every second.

● In Ontario, Canada, the Sudbury Neutrino Observatory is buried 2,000 metres underground. It collects neutrinos for study using a ball-shaped tank 12 metres across containing a special type of water, called 'heavy water'.

How we Explore the Sun

More than one hundred space satellites and probes have taken pictures of the Sun or sent back information about its size and structure, its movements and the energy it pours out.

Sun-exploring craft

Several spacecraft have studied the Sun, including *SOHO*, *Solar-Max* and *Genesis*. In 2003 *SOHO* suffered an antenna (aerial) problem, but this was fixed and the craft continues to send back information.

Another space probe is *Ulysses*, launched in 1990 from the US space shuttle. Most telescopes and spacecraft view the Sun from the side, as we see it from Earth. *Ulysses'* task was to study the Sun's top and bottom – its North and South Poles.

Ulysses first travelled out to the gigantic planet Jupiter, in 1992. Jupiter's huge gravity made the craft curve around and down, and then back towards the centre of the Solar System. It passed under the Sun, over its South Pole, around its far side, then up and over its North Pole, and out again to Jupiter. *Ulysses* has done this twice, in 1994-95 and 2000-01. A third visit is planned for 2007-2008.

Ulysses *has foil blankets to protect against the heat of the Sun and the intense cold out near Jupiter.*

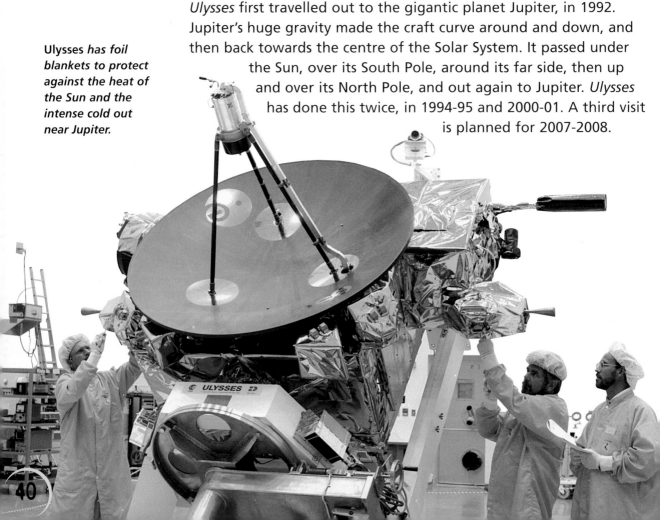

Ulysses is about the size of a large car and weighs as much as six adult people. It does not take pictures. But it carries equipment to detect the Sun's magnetic field and various types of dust and particles passing through space, including the solar wind and fragments of plasma.

ACE mission

The *ACE* (*Advanced Composition Explorer*) satellite was launched in 1997. It is designed to study the Sun's atmosphere of the chromosphere and corona, and also its high-energy cosmic rays and the solar wind. *ACE* can help to predict when 'magnetic storms' on the Sun may affect power lines and communications here on Earth.

Satellites far above the clouds, dust and atmosphere of Earth see the Sun much more clearly than ground telescopes.

Strange orbit

ACE is in orbit 1.5 million kilometres from Earth, towards the Sun. But it does not go around the Earth or another physical object. It travels around an empty place in space where the gravity of the Earth and Sun exactly balance each other. This is called the L1 libration (Lagrangian) point. The *SOHO* satellite is in a similar 'halo' orbit.

Space exploration

The Sun's immense pull of gravity has been both a problem and a help over the years for deep-space probes on long journeys. The probes have been aimed so that after one part of their trip, they pass near the Sun. Its gravity pulls them around on a new course, which means they can head into a different part of the Solar System.

Space Facts

The Helios spacecraft

● *Helios 1* launched in 1974, and *Helios 2* in 1976. At their closest they passed within about 45 million kilometres of the Sun.

● The *Helios* probes also became the fastest human-made objects ever, travelling at about a quarter of a million kilometres per second as they swung around the Sun.

● Both craft carried about 10 sets of equipment to measure the solar wind, the Sun's magnetism, various kinds of waves and rays, and tiny bits of rock called micrometeoroids whizzing through space.

The Future

More than a dozen spacecraft are currently studying the Sun in great detail, and further missions are planned over the next few years. The information they gather not only extends our knowledge of the Sun itself, and of space in general. It also has uses here on Earth, including a possible source of clean, plentiful energy for the future.

Two views

STEREO, the Solar TErrestrial RElations Observatory, is actually two very similar spacecraft. Both follow the same path as Earth around the Sun. But one *STEREO* is slightly in front of our planet and the other just behind. They take pictures of Sun events at the same time from different views, and combine them into one 3D (three-dimensional) view. This is similar to how we use our two eyes to give a 3D view, so we can see depth and judge distance.

STEREO will focus especially on coronal mass ejections, CMEs, when 10 billion tonnes of matter, energy and magnetism leave the Sun at more than two million kilometres per hour as a giant 'bubble' (see page 29). If a CME heads for Earth, *STEREO* can give warning of the damage it might cause to power lines, electricity supplies, satellites, radio and communication links.

No human has ever seen this sunrise. The wheeled rover Spirit *took the photograph at dawn on planet Mars.*

Space probes such as Ulysses will continue to uncover the Sun's secrets, bringing information that has practical uses here on Earth.

Energy for Earth

In one second the Sun gives off almost a million times more energy than everyone on Earth uses in a whole year. As scientists come to understand how the energy is formed, they may also find ways of trapping it. Giant 'solar sails' in space could receive the Sun's light and other radiation (rays and waves), and send it down to Earth in some form of energy beam.

Fusion power

Another approach is to create conditions in the core of the Sun, here on our planet. Nuclear power on Earth comes from splitting apart bits of atoms, called nuclear fission. An alternative is to copy the Sun by using nuclear fusion (see page 19). A few test reactors have been built, shaped like giant doughnuts. They contain superheated plasma held in place by powerful magnetism. Nuclear fusion has happened in these reactors. But the energy put in to create the plasma is far more than the energy that comes out.

Space Facts

Scientists' predictions

- The Sun is about halfway through its total lifetime of around 10 billion years.

- Scientists think that it will probably start to get bigger and redder, a couple of billion years from now.

- Eventually the Sun may be so large that its surface reaches out to Earth. (However Earth may well not be here – it could have been boiled into vapour or forced away into deep space.)

- The Sun's outer layers will shred away and fly off into space.

- Finally the Sun will become a small, cool star called a white dwarf, which gradually fades away.

Timeline of Discovery

2,450 years ago   Anaxagoras suggested the Sun was burning rock or metal, not a god's chariot drawn across the sky, and was threatened with death.

2,000 years ago   Chinese astronomers made official records of sunspots.

1300s AD   Aztec people in Central America began human sacrifices to their Sun god Huitzilopochtli.

1543   Nicolaus Copernicus's book suggested that the Earth and other planets went around the Sun, rather than the Earth being the centre of everything.

1610   Sunspots were first seen through a telescope by Johannes and David Fabricius, then by Galileo.

1672   Jean Richer and Giovanni Domenico Cassini made the first fairly accurate measurement of the Sun's distance from Earth, the astronomical unit, AU.

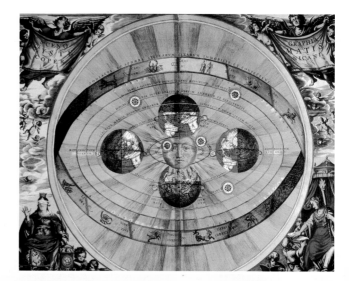

An illustration of the theory put forward by Nicolaus Copernicus.

1684   The French Academy of Sciences made improved measurements of the AU.

1814   Joseph von Fraunhofer noticed dark lines when sunlight was split into its separate colours of the spectrum.

1859   Gustav Kirchhoff showed that the dark lines revealed the chemical make-up of the Sun.

1859   Solar flares were first observed, by Richard Carrington.

1939   Hans Bethe worked out how the Sun makes energy in its core by nuclear fusion.

1959 The space probe *Luna 1* made the first accurate measurements of the solar wind.

1962 The McMath Solar Telescope, later renamed the McMath-Pierce Solar Telescope, was established at Kitt Peak National Observatory, Arizona, USA.

1962 The first in a long series of Earth-orbiting, Sun-studying satellites, the *OSOs* or *Orbiting Solar Observatories*, was launched.

1971 The first coronal mass ejection (CME) was detected by *OSO-7*, the seventh *Orbiting Solar Observatory*.

1974 Launch of Helios 1.

1976 Launch of Helios 2.

1990 The *Ulysses* probe was launched from the space shuttle, to study the Sun's North and South Poles.

1995 The joint European/US probe *SOHO* was launched.

1997 The *ACE* (*Advanced Composition Explorer*) satellite was launched.

The SOHO satellite is the size of a car.

2001 The space probe *Genesis* set off to capture samples of the solar wind.

2002 The small spacecraft *RHESSI* was launched to study the Sun's outpourings of energy.

2004 On 8 September *Genesis* returned to Earth but was damaged on crash-landing.

2005 Early results were announced from the *Genesis* mission.

2006 Launch of the *STEREO* twin satellites to obtain 3D (three-dimensional) images of the Sun and especially CMEs.

Glossary

astronomer A scientist who specializes in the study of space.

astronomical Unit (AU) The average distance from the Earth to the Sun, which is 149,597,870 (almost 150 million) km.

chromosphere The layer of gases around the Sun, just above its surface.

convective zone The layer of the Sun between the radiative zone and the photosphere.

core (solar core) The centre or middle of the Sun, where matter changes into energy by nuclear fusion.

corona The vast outermost, wispy layer of the Sun, that extends far into space.

eclipse When one object in space moves into the shadow of another, such as a solar eclipse, when the Moon comes between the Sun and Earth.

Fraunhofer lines Dark lines in the band of rainbow-like colours made by splitting the Sun's light into its spectrum.

galaxy A massive group or clump of stars with empty space around them.

geocentric A version of the Solar System where the other planets and the Sun go around the Earth, which is now known to be incorrect.

gravity A pulling or attracting force possessed by all objects, mass and matter.

heliocentric A version of the Solar System where all the planets go around the Sun, which is known to be correct.

mass Matter or substance, in terms of the numbers and types of atoms or other tiny particles.

nebula A huge wispy, flimsy 'cloud' of dust, gases and other tiny particles floating in space.

observatory (astronomical observatory) A building or place, usually with telescopes and similar equipment, where people study objects in space.

orbit The path of one object going around another.

photosphere The surface of the Sun that we see from Earth.

radiation Energy that spreads out or radiates from its source, often in the form of rays or waves.

radiative zone The layer around the Sun's core, where energy travels mainly as rays and waves of radiation.

solar To do with the Sun.

star A space object that changes matter to energy and gives this off as light, heat and other kinds of waves and rays.

transit When one object in space passes in front of another and looks much smaller than the farther object.

Further Information

Books

The Sun and Moon (Exploring the Universe)
Robin Kerrod Raintree, 2001

The Sun Ron Miller, 21st Century, 2002

A Look at the Sun (Out of This World)
Ray Spangenburg and Kit Moser
Franklin Watts, 2002

Amazing Sun (Amazing World)
Neil Morris
School Specialty Publishing, 2006

National Geographic Encyclopedia of Space
Linda K Glover
National Geographic Society, 2005

Organizations

National Aeronautics & Space
Administration (NASA)
Organization that runs the US space program
www.nasa.gov

European Space Agency (ESA)
Organization responsible for space flight
and exploration by European countries
www.esa.int

International Astronomical Union (IAU)
The official world astronomy organization,
responsible for naming stars, planets,
moons and other objects in space
www.iau.org

Jet Propulsion Laboratory (JPL)
Centre responsible for NASA's robot space
probes
www.jpl.nasa.gov

The Planetary Society
Organization devoted to the exploration of
the Solar System
www.planetary.org

Websites

http://www.noao.edu/outreach/kptour
/mcmath.html
Official site of the world's largest Sun-
studying telescope

http://solarsystem.jpl.nasa.gov/planets/
profile.cfm?Object=Sun
Facts and figures about the Sun from NASA

http://sohowww.nascom.nasa.gov/
Official site of the SOHO satellite

http://www.kidsastronomy.com/
our_sun.htm
The Sun's pages on a large website with
plenty of fun information on many space
topics

http://www.nasa.gov/worldbook/sun_world
book.html
A more complicated site with many details
about the Sun

http://www.nasa.gov/vision/universe/solarsys
tem/sun_earthday2006.html
NASA photographs and videos of solar
eclipses

http://www.parkes.atnf.csiro.au/
Information on the huge Parkes Radio
Telescope near Alectown, about 365
kilometres west of Sydney, Australia.

Index

Numbers in **bold** indicate pictures.

THE EARTH AND SPACE

Contents of titles in the series:

WAYLAND